...s boat

by Ben Butterworth
pictures by Lorraine Calaora

Nelson

'My arms are worn out,' Father said.

'My legs are worn out,' Trog said.

'My arms **and** my legs are worn out,'
said Grandpa Gripe,
'**and** I have fallen off the log
three times.'

Father, Mother, Trog and Grandpa
were sitting on the log boat
and paddling it down the river.
It was very hard work.

'The Quickerwits go on the river,'
Mother said to Father.
'They are not worn out like this.
Trog, go and see what they do.'

'Right,' Trog said.

Trog went over the hills
and over the rivers
to the land of the Quickerwits.

'We are worn out
with paddling our boat,' Trog said.
'What do you do?'

'It's easy,' the Quickerwits said.
'It's very easy.
We don't paddle at all.
We are never worn out.
We put a sail on the boat!'

Back went Trog to Father,
Mother and Grandpa Gripe.

'It's easy,' Trog said.
'I shall put a sail on the boat.
No more paddling for me.'

'Good,' Grandpa said.
'That's very good!'

8

Trog put a sail
on the boat and
went with Father
up and down the river.
Then Mother went
for a sail with Trog.
'Well, it is easy,'
Grandpa said.
'I will have a go
tomorrow.'

The next day
Grandpa said, 'Now, watch me.'
'But the wind is strong today,'
Trog said to him.
'Good,' Grandpa said.
'The wind will be
too strong for you,' said Father.
'Don't be silly,' Grandpa said.
'The stronger the wind is
the faster I shall go.'
He jumped onto the boat
and set off.

The wind blew stronger
and stronger.
Grandpa went faster
and faster.

'Help!
Help!' he yelled.
'I can't stop
this thing.'

The wind blew the boat
down the river,
on and on,
past the land
of the Quickerwits.

'Help me! Save me!'
Grandpa shouted.
'I can't stop.'

I can't swim!

The wind was so strong
that the boat tipped right over.
Grandpa Gripe
was tipped into the river.

'Save me!' he shouted.
'I can't swim!'

The Quickerwits
came swimming out to Grandpa
and saved him.

'That's a fast boat,'
they said to him.
'Did you like sailing?'

'Did I like sailing?' Grandpa said.
'Paddling wore my arms out
and paddling wore my legs out.
Sailing nearly killed me.
You can have all the boats you like.

I'm going to **walk**.'